WINGLESS DREAMER PUBLISHER

Roots
&
Rivers

Forewings

Thorax

Hindwings

Filament

Anther

Nectar-Sac

Edited by Shreya Mishra and
Ruchi Acharya

$\bar{A}$

$R = \sqrt{A^2 + B^2 + 2AB\cos\theta}$

$\tan\alpha = \dfrac{B\sin\theta}{}$

Wingless Dreamer

UPLIFTING WRITERS AND ARTISTS THROUGH OUR CREATIVE COMMUNITY

Thank you so much for all your efforts and support that you gave to me in past few months. I'm very happy to receive the book as it is my first time when my poem got published and I want thought to show my gratitude to you through this mail. Hope we get to work together again in the future and wishing you all the best for future endeavours.- Mitali Prasad

I'm literally in tears right now, oh my God. Thanks you @winglessdreamerlit !! The books arrived and are AMAZINGLY FANTASTIC! The cover art is beautiful, the collections stunning! I am filled with such surprise and honor my pieces were published with you, it makes me the happiest lassie in the world. Thank you so much!! If you want to support on of the best publishers EVER, go to Winglessdreamer.com or search their books on Amazon! So grateful. -Gratia Serpento

Hi there, I just wanted to say that after reading some of the poetry on Wingless Dreamer, I feel inspired and in awe. I've been writing on and off as a hobby for a few years now but seeing what you've done and how you've built this whole community of writers, I'm really inspired and impressed. You've given me just a bit more inspiration to keep working on my projects and for that I thank you.- Ryan

Best of afternoons! I am simply sending this email to first thank you for this as I am truly humbled by your decision to accept this poem for publication. I wrote this poem after many nights of night terrors and panic attacks due to my looming anxiety over the pandemic and instant changes the world is going through seemingly overnight. Your validation of this poem is received by such validation and a feeling of triumph that I cannot put into words, so genuinely, thank you. -Arnaldo Batista

I am most excited to receive this new book, and I have already shared your various publications with many friends and family! I am very happy to have come across your publication and look forward to reading many more of your other contributor's pieces!- Natalie Kormos

I shall be anxiously awaiting the book's arrival. I always appreciate your editing efforts. They have always been terrific in the past. More book graphics sounds great, I'm excited to see what they are all about. I'm going to your website now and check out what else you have going on, I know you always have a lot going on. You folks are a great publisher in my book, and I'm not just saying that because you've published some of my work, I sincerely mean it and my family and friends agree. Keep up the great work that you do, I know you will.-William David

Keep up this excellent work. Poetry truly connects the readers with poetic souls across countries and cultures – Amita Sanghvi

It is a great joy for me that a kindhearted editor of a journal like you has liked my poem. Thank you again. Be happy in life this is my heartfelt wishes to you.-Sandip Saha

There is such a positive vibes from Wingless Dreamer, unlike any other publisher. -Gavin Bourke

It's an honor and a privilege to be part of the most eminent Literary Journal of the young minds 'Wingless Dreamer.' This is a place where dreams becomes reality. Wingless Dreamer has made possible for all poets & readers to flap the wings of dreams, imagination & aspiration into the deep blue sky of peace, progress & prosperity. You may prosper like the locket of Apollo. You may win unnumbered hearts of poet lovers in future. – Mr. Saheb SK

ROOTS AND RIVERS

Edited and compiled by

Shreya Mishra

Ruchi Acharya

ABOUT US

In 2019, Indian author Ruchi Acharya dreamed of a literary community that could bridge the gap between fellow, emerging writers with a fervent passion to create and the world of traditional publishing. She envisioned a place where writers and artists are allowed to publish based solely on the merit of their creative skills. Her desire and inspired vision culminated in the design of Wingless Dreamer Publisher, a forum providing aspiring and experienced creators alike the opportunity to share their love of English literature and art on a global platform.

Throughout the year, our Wingless Dreamer team offers a multitude of themed writing contests designed to stimulate fresh ideas and present an opportunity for talented authors worldwide to contribute perspectives through creative expression efforts. We select the best of the best submissions and stream together the components of writing, editing, and illustrating to result in publications of beautiful literary anthologies that we promote in the marketplace. Our commitment to providing this single platform and process allows our authors and artists to bypass challenges and obstacles associated with the traditional publishing goal, and instead maintain their focus and devotion to creating works of art.

Most meaningful is that Wingless Dreamer community members become part of a family, and are guided, encouraged, and supported as they take each step toward cultivating a successful writing or art career. Non-native English-speaking authors are also granted access to free reviews, critiques, marketing, and, in some cases, funding for their work. Our community has slowly, but steadily, grown to become a prominent stage featuring well-known professional writers and artists from all over the world.

Finally, we at Wingless Dreamer are devoted to publishing poetry, fiction, and artwork reflecting the entirety of multiple perspectives and varied experiences extracted from the deep well of soulful human existence. As such, BIPOC, LGBTQ, disabled, minority, and other marginalized voices are especially invited to join in the sharing. Our ultimate goal is to uplift the human spirit through a diverse creative community. At its core, the human spirit desires connections through expressions. We ardently endeavor to gift wings to these heartfelt dreams.

FOUNDER'S PEN

Being a writer can sometimes be solitary and quiet. A writer can understand how it feels to fall in love with every single character, battle with dialogues, work with vivid poetic devices, endeavor for perfection, and build an entire universe from scratch. Guess what? You're not alone. We understand the efforts you put every day into your work. Since we are a team of writers and artists too.

The writing industry is always considered as something obscure and profound by the public in general. It has become so difficult to stand alone and to stick with a writing career in the commercial society we live in today. Compared to other financial and economic-related jobs, things related to writing are the minority.

Writing is a terrific passion, and writers work in a hard industry, one where success is often sought and little received. Writing is not merely something we do, but something we are, and that makes it one of the most challenging of all pursuits in life.

I never got the right support to become a writer at the prime youth of my life. In the place where I come from writing is considered a cute hobby instead of passion - a commitment that writers made to themselves. Writers don't receive the same respect that other professions do. It's quite condescending. That sort of mentality is also so harmful to amateur writers' confidence. From my past experience, I realize that this issue needs to be addressed.

People need to understand that writing is a hard business. It is time-consuming and after dedicating late-night hours, a roller coaster of emotions to finally produce a piece of literary work that might be read around the globe.

So, I come up with this publishing company and yeah I am proud of it.

In the end, I would like to urge all the people who are reading this to never ever give up on your dreams. Seize the day. Every day counts. I hope you will support us and encourage our team efforts. More power to your pen. Cheers! -*Ruchi Acharya, Wingless Dreamer Founder*

OUR JUDGE'S MESSAGE

Judging for Roots and River has been such an incredible experience. Each piece felt like its own world, pulling me into places, emotions, and moments I'd never thought to imagine. I loved getting to live in these snapshots, experiencing lives and situations so different from my own. Congratulations to everyone who made it into the anthology! It was inspiring to see how each writer brought something unique to the table. Thank you all for sharing these journeys!

Warm regards,
Shreya Mishra

ABOUT THE JUDGE, SHREYA MISHRA

Meet Shreya Mishra, she is a blend of passion and purpose, seamlessly weaving the worlds of medicine and content creation. Her love for music and dance infuses rhythm into her life, while her compassionate spirit guides her journey toward healing and expression. Every step she takes resonates with curiosity and creativity, inspiring those around her with her warmth and determination.

CONTENT

Winner for the Roots and Rivers Contest 2024 🏆 - Grand winner 🏆 - First runner-up 🏆 - Second runner-up 🎖 - Top Finalists

1. AURORA

Upon the dark canvas of night,
the universe paints in brushes of luminescence,
each ribbon of light a soft stroke across the heavens,
shivers of violet, cascades of green fire,
a celestial waltz woven of solar winds.

This magnetic display of boundless beauty,
this cosmic quilt of pulsing aurora,
drapes down fingers of light, embracing me.

Sighing in time with nature's breath,
I imagine this is how it feels
to be held by you.

AMEYTHIST MORELAND

Ameythist Moreland holds a B.S. with concentrations in English, language, and health from Western Michigan University. She is the author of two new-adult science fiction novels and an emerging poet whose work has been featured in Wingless Dreamers Books' Night Worship collection, the Poet's Choice Seven Jumbled Words anthology, as well as From Whispers to Roars arts & literary magazine. Her passion for the written word continues to drive her creative pursuits.

2. SUPERB BIRD-OF-PARADISE

Your paradise is mottled with my pupils.
Along, within, my streams of teal iron,
dancing, dueling ultramarines, and mossing,
your quintessential white hour
is my mountainous, clear, dual beat and stand;
so lift reflections like wings
and see they are useless without your earth—
offering, quartz-bearing shift,
where you grip the mud like torrential sand.

You are ever the land in-between
night and day, upon the traversing bough
upon which you watch both of mine.
I attempt to impress not only love,
but your lifetime audience of gemmed gifts,
with a display only the scaled
aqueous could pull off; gravity
cannot compete with the true us.

I am the amenable, laving eyes
in the middle of the night and sea;
so store your preeminence, for my acquiescence
may just overwhelm the boughs.

My fervour may just leave you bereft
of fresh water, as it soughs it as the sea,
farther downward, away from propinquity.
Paradise was direct, exigent as the line of sight.
Paradise was synonymous with water.
Where are we now, in front of the bluing art?

My fervour may just leave you bereft
of fresh water, as it soughs it as the sea,
farther downward, away from
propinquity.
-Dan Lockeridge

DAN LOCKERIDGE

Daniel Lockeridge is a thirty-year-old Australian who has self-published a series of poetry consisting of three collections. He has had poetry and prose publications in Gasher Press, Literary Revelations, Quillkeepers Press, Querencia Press, The Winged Moon Magazine, and Reverie Magazine, among others.

3. SURRENDER, AN ODE TO WYOMING

Here again, at home,
majesty of alpine meadow and winding trail,
the mountains who held me close,
cathedral of return,
a glassy cradle,
closer to the woman of tomorrow,
a back aching with growing pains,
the sloping saviors
who taught me how to breathe.

This poem is dedicated to the women
who saw scared and uncertain,
loose bones and a heavy heart,
and said, "Powerful and strong,
watch, how your body
can move mountains,
how big you can become,
a giant in granite caverns.
You are physically capable of more
than your mind can comprehend yet,
so trust the ground beneath your feet,
trust your step.
You are in control of your body,
and it is beautiful."

Burned-out muscles and muddy boots,
to one foot in front of the other,
because faith can take
shape as an alpine lake,
a gasp, shriek of joy at the freeze,
pinch and pull beneath your ribs
as you come up for air.
You are everywhere
in the song of your heart,
and what a privilege
it is to feel.

Orchestra of stars,
to crackling embers, the night's slow leak
into tears, belly-aching laughter, and peace,
the pocket of calm, of surrender,
in the shadow, sheer size of mountains.

There is a whole world dancing
at the tip of your tongue.
Speak into the
wind: "I belong here,
I am at home in myself,
and I will wander,
wander on."

\

KAITLIN WEISS

Kaitlin Weiss (she/her) is a 22-year-old poet based in New Jersey. She is a senior at Bowdoin College majoring in Government and Legal Studies and Africana Studies. Her two greatest loves are performing spoken word poetry and leading backpacking and hiking trips for teens.

4. THICKETS OF YELLOWSTONE

Between weaving pines,
so thick light scarcely splints through,
a pair of antlers rise like fractured timber,

bare of velvet, weathered bone,
worn satin by tireless seasons
of thunder and verglas.

The elk idles silent, head held high,
its breath rises in hazy clouds,
faint to the early chill.

Pupils shutter wide,
dark as deep-rushing rivers
where streams converge.

It watches from a distance,
a gaze that holds
the weight of an old world,

one that knows the tang
of fiery dawn and smoke-risen dusk,
the slow pull of roots
aching from a newlywed frost.

In a passing moment,
it flees amongst ivy greens,
leaving the forest to remember.

In a passing moment,
it flees amongst ivy greens,
leaving the forest to remember.
-Claire Kroening

CLAIRE KROENING

Claire Kroening is an award-winning poet and writer based in the upper midwest. Their work has appeared in a multitude of publications worldwide, including Vellichor Literary Magazine, Young Writers Journal, and Bitter Melon Review. When not working on their latest endeavors, they appreciate visiting art museums and exploring the coastlines.

5. BLESSING THE DEAD MONARCH

She leaves for the south,
never to see home again.
The winds are at her back.
Red rock valleys roll and release
into the unfurled fields and flowers.
The Great Plains stretch out to define
the sawtooth Appalachian mountains.
Her message has a mighty meaning.
She signals health and happiness.
Hers is a journey, says to all,
Fertile is the future.
She rests on the corn plant.
A chemical rain descends.
Blisters begin on the wings.
The burning knocks her down.
Her flight falls furiously.
Her antennae curl over her eyes.
Tumbling and crashing,
her migration, invisible.

He headed to the north,
leaving a sailor's life,
his family's fishing ship—
an empty catch.
Searching for a home,
a white ghost forest watches him
walk.
Concerned from the grave,
their roots, ocean-salted.
On day thirty, his breath shortens.
He lies on the ground,
sees the burnt butterfly, eye to eye.
He buries the dead monarch,
dirt over the wings,
blesses her and thinks,
We are all foreign somewhere.

Searching for a home,
a white ghost forest watches him walk.
Concerned from the grave,
their roots, ocean-salted.

-Hope Cotter

HOPE COTTER

Hope Cotter is an author and writer. She is a graduate of New York University. She lives in Hopewell, NJ, with her husband, three sons, and peacock. She has been published in Red Door, Wingless Dreamer, Poets Choice, and other publications. She loves the smell of old books and new ideas.

6. 까마귀 (THE CROW)

"The crows sound different here than back home,"
a friend remarked on our walk down the hill from work.
It was almost cherry blossom season,
and the trees were anxiously waiting for their chance to bloom,
before the petals would float and fall and wither,
only to bloom all over again.

The crow above us continued to laugh,
seemingly not with us, but at us.
My friend then told me about an app called Merlin,
where you can identify bird sounds,
thanks to the wonderful minds of Cornell.

Her sister, a bird watcher, came to visit in South Korea
and felt overjoyed by all of the different birds here.
She spent her mornings cataloguing new birds
and her evenings comparing birds here to the ones in Louisiana.
Simple as it was, it was something that never really occurred to me—
how the same bird could sound so distinct in different places.

Just like that, suddenly, it struck me:
I was living somewhere new.
It wasn't the food or the language or the people,
but the birds, that made me realize it.
Do the crows, too, know I've moved to this new country?
When they hear me talk, do they try to identify me, too?
Is their laugh simply a sign of confusion, of delight?
Just as I view the crows as foreign, am I foreign to them, too?

It was another day walking down the hill,
now nearing the end of cherry blossom season.
The petals had fallen, smattering the ground
in a sea of white and blush.
Amidst our small talk, there was the crow,
laughing again.

And rather than reaching for Merlin,
I learned simply to laugh back.

BROOKE DALY

Brooke Daly was born and raised in Orlando, Florida. She graduated in 2022 from Emory University, where she majored in German Studies, English, and Creative Writing. Daly's work has been published in Bridge: the Bluffton University Literary Journal and Stonecrop Magazine. She is inspired by writers such as Yoko Tawada, who question the bounds and functions of language and relate these questions to their personal lives. She worked as a Fulbright English Teaching Assistant in Germany for the 2022-2023 school year and now teaches in Busan, South Korea. She enjoys writing in English, German, and Korean, often mixing all three together. She hopes that her writing, whether plays, poetry, or nonfiction, can resonate with readers and provide a place for rest and laughter.

7. BOY OF WONDER

I once knew a boy filled with wonder.

He would look toward the earthy
soils of his mother's garden
and watch as the ants traverse their urban jungle,
in search of their next meal.

He would look out to the horizon
of a quiet lake, deep in the woods,
and notice each ripple emanating
from a water strider.

He would gaze at the star-laden sky for hours,
imagining what possibilities lie beyond our planet
and the dismay at knowing he was born too early for answers.

The boy was often told
he asked too many questions.

And eventually, the boy lost his wonder.

Maybe it's under the concrete streets,

buried deep under the city and the subway.
Maybe it's hidden in the stars,
behind the luminous haze from streetlights and skyscrapers.

But one fateful day,
he decided to look down,
and he saw a dandelion growing
between the cracks of the sidewalk.
A curious sensation arose from deep within him,
a familiar feeling he thought was lost.

He thought to himself,

"How could something so small and so fragile
reach up and rebel against human hegemony?"

And he realized his wonder is not gone,
but resurrected once more.

He would look toward the earthy
soils of his mother's garden
and watch as the ants traverse their urban jungle,
in search of their next meal.
-Christian Loyo

CHRISTIAN LOYO

Christian Loyo is a PhD candidate in the Department of Biology at the Massachusetts Institute of Technology, where he studies how bacteria defend themselves against bacterial viruses, known as bacteriophages. He is a Chicano scientist and poet and sees these two disciplines as ways of understanding the world we live in. He was previously featured as a scientist in "The Poetry of Science," which aims to increase the representation of Black, Indigenous, Latinx, Asian, Pacific Islander, and People of Color's lived experiences in poetry, photography, and the sciences.

8. ULMUS

The tree that she clung to was a twisted, diseased, shriveled thing.
Long ago, it stood as a proud sentinel in the yard of the family's house,
yet the years had been hard.
As shouts rang from the house, she shivered,
and her trembles sent a cascade of shriveled leaves spiraling down.
A beetle scuttled across the bark near her fingertips, unnoticed.
Looking over her shoulder at the family home,
she felt no pull to it, nor to the people inside.
She would go, not away, but up, up, up
the broken branches of the sickened tree.
As she climbed, her shoes chipped away at the bark,
revealing red streaks in the wood.
The spindly branches should break,
and yet they supported her weight.
Then, finally, once high in the sky,
she looked back at the place that she came from.
For the first time, it didn't hurt her to see the house.

$$d = \sqrt{(x_2 - x_1)^2 + (y_2 - y_1)^2}$$

$$V = s^3$$

The tree that she clung to was a twisted, diseased, shriveled thing. Long ago, it stood as a proud sentinel in the yard of the family's house, yet the years had been hard.

-Erica Berquist

$$V = \tfrac{4}{3}\pi r^3$$

$CH_4 + 2O_2$

ERICA BERQUIST

Since graduating from Towson University in 2014 with a BS in English, Erica Lee Berquist has worked for KnowledgeWorks Global Ltd. as an editorial associate and Cloudmed Solutions LLC as a recovery analyst. Grub Street Literary Magazine's volumes 65 and 71, Levitate Magazine issue 7, Sheepshead Review's Spring 2023 Edition, OFIC Magazine issue 6, German Poems anthology by Poet's Choice, Marathon Literary Review issue 24, and Nat 1's anthology Star-Crossed and Other Tales of Intergalactic Love have all published Erica's work. In her free time, she enjoys making jewellery, researching family history for herself and others, gardening, and spending time with her cats.

9. AN ECOSYSTEM

So, the rocks have kicked me out their ranks again.
I failed to still along the banks with the will they show.

I know, I know,
My mind throws itself over, like wind,
My lips trip over words like rivers,
Foaming softly, effusive in the moment.

At the bend, I slow,
Flow grown so thick with leaning pines,
Who shadow me with reaching hopes.

I've lined myself with truths,
Each spreading room housing new tunes.
Moon advancing my actions,
Satisfaction not a singular thing for me,
But a whole ecosystem.

I want to know each role intimately,
But some born-with abilities
Made me deny experiences.
Some bound-to beliefs heed to shade,
Like ferns who probably yearn for supple sun,
But live coupled in the cool of yesterday.

At the delta,
The spoken grows big and open,
Mouth so relieved to announce change,
It forgets the guilt of myriad stones,
Filed down into silt, built into reserves.

Will eroded by eternity,
Eventually cast out to sea,
Like me and my myopic nerves,
Traversing shore to shore,
Longing for more.

Will eroded by eternity,
Eventually cast out to sea,
Like me and my myopic nerves,
Traversing shore to shore,
Longing for more.
-Corrie Thompson

CORRIE THOMPSON

Corrie Thompson is a poet and photographer from the suburbs outside Chicago. Her writing appears in Eclectica Magazine, Mantis, In Parentheses, Poet's Choice, Good Life Literary Journal, Haiku Journal, and Flash Fiction Magazine. She would love to become a birch tree in her next life and be one with the natural world she loves so much.

10. KINDLING: TWIGS TO IGNITE A PIECE OF WRITING

My granddaughter told me, "Here, Grandma, plant these." And I did. Now you've got to lean back to see the top of her tree.

I taught her brother to climb trees, but not to climb sticky pine sap. Someone told me, "You shouldn't have to use a weed-wacker on your gutters."

Looking out my window one morning, I didn't remember a branch being there. It fell on the roof. My Hmong neighbor cut it down for me.

The walnuts that fell from the black walnut tree were not edible.

Some people complain when their silver maple tree drops its leaves.

A neighbor complained to the City of my branches to my buffer zone. Without warning, the City cut down a shady boulevard tree,

whose canopy protected, provided needed shade. Squirrels chase round trees; birds chatter.

Newspapers, writing paper, pencils, wood excelsior, sawdust were all trees. I was born in the fall, when leaves fall, not a bridge fall.

My first drawing was a pine cone. My first remembered song lyrics were, *"Primrose Lane."*

"Will the row of pine trees grow overnight?" we asked. "No. They will take 15-20 years." A nearby college cut down trees to make a basketball court.

"What does this teach students!?" I'm guilty, too; my dining room table, a futon-couch, are oak.

Like the profligate cutting down of trees for Christmas décor. Trees have colors and consistencies: some hard, some not. There's a young oak tree on my way to the library, precariously close to the sidewalk. Shall I dig it up in a midnight run?

ELIZABETH WADSWORTH ELLIS

Elizabeth's work is currently published in Literary Reviews.

11. TREES POKED THROUGH MY SALAD

Trees poked through my salad last night.
You said my charging phone looked like a toy 2001 monolith. Now,
with streaming TV, all catastrophe is local.
We want cars we can't afford, though our shoulders won't fit through
their gas spouts.
The truth is, I never leave my desk. Last week, Mother Nature changed
the world.

LAWRENCE BRIDGES

Lawrence Bridges' poetry has appeared in The New Yorker, Poetry, and Tampa Review. He has published three volumes of poetry: Horses on Drums (Red Hen Press, 2006), Flip Days (Red Hen Press, 2009), and Brownwood (Tupelo Press, 2016).

12. RAFT

At first, when I was water,
dissatisfied with storms and swells, with how
a squall could whip up out of nowhere
and thrust my slumbering surface skyward,
undulating—I looked for a raft.
Always a perception of listing,
as if the sea itself could capsize and feared itself,
so that even when the horizon was a line
to infinity, I still looked for a raft.
I found many along the way, and I clung
to each and worked to forget my watery nature,
sometimes for years, decades even.
I drifted, splashed and salty, sunbaked.
The rough-hewn buoy, though, was a story,
a gripping story that kept me floating
in a dream of wood and steel,
that kept me believing I was of those things,
those things forged and bound,
as if anything real would be so hard and lonely,
as if anything worth preserving would want
me to cling to it.

At first, when I was water,
dissatisfied with storms and swells, with
how
a squall could whip up out of nowhere
and thrust my slumbering surface
skyward,
-Lyall Harris

LYALL HARRIS

Lyall Harris is a visual artist and writer whose poetry and prose have appeared in The Minnesota Review, The New Guard, The Dewdrop, The Perch Magazine, The Vincent Brothers Review, Prose Online, and elsewhere. Her book-length poem Barrier Island is forthcoming from The Black Spring Press Group. www.lyallharris.com.

13. SAFETY

Morocco, a bus with broken windows and night.
The cold is seeping in through my thin jacket, I am expecting.
Warmed by my husband, I don't think about the hardships that could
befall me. In my youth, so much confidence – and then – fears breed
like the cockroaches in my childhood's apartments.

Sri Lanka, already with my son, we stop in a reserve, and I need to get
into the bush in a very Lithuanian way – away from sight. I step on a
huge snake; I forget what I came for. And then – slowly – I start to see
the world, a scary but magnificent place. I don't know, who will
prevail. I'm afraid of the tropics, their mosquitoes and the diseases they
carry. I'm afraid of dengue fever and malaria drugs – the last time I
took them, I was writing goodbye letters. The cows on the road, a
twisted peddler and boys in a dark cave grasping my breasts – the
world is a terrible but magnificent place.

When I start to fear my own forest and the wolf in it, I understand,
that I should remember Madike's mother, who realized how dangerous
life here can be at home, in cozy Junibaken.

*When I start to fear my own forest and
the wolf in it, I understand,
that I should remember Madike's
mother, who realized how dangerous
life here can be at home, in cozy
Junibaken.*
-LINA BUIVIDAVICIUTE

LINA BUIVIDAVICIUTE

Lina Buividavičiūtė was born on May 14, 1986. She is a poet and literary critic. Lina is the author of two poetry books in the Lithuanian language. Her poetry is published in "Matter," "Masters," "Proverse Poetry Prize" contest anthologies, "Drunk Monkeys," "Beyond Words," "The Dewdrop," "The Limit Experience," "Poets Choice," "HOW," "Beyond Queer Words," "Maudlin House," "Cathexis Northwest Press," "Poetry Online" magazines, and "Versopolis" poetry platform. Upcoming publications will appear in "New millennium writings," "Cathexis Northwest Press," "Quillkeepers Press," "The Stardust Review," and "Beyond Words" magazine.

14. FLUTTERBYS

dandelion lace
of wings gone flounce,
that bounce from purple
bulb to spring-leafed stem,
will trace
the field for nectar's taste
and fly like feathers
whipped by wind,
the silent motor,
mystic thirst
quenched by
film of drizzled day.

no photograph,
no human gaze
may capture
passing passion flown,
a flap, a flame, a chiffon
graze
that jerks about
yet defines grace.

dandelion lace
of wings gone flounce,
that bounce from purple
bulb to spring-leafed stem,
-Tamra Plotnick

TAMRA PLOTNICK

Tamra Plotnick's poetry and prose works have been published in many journals and anthologies, including Serving House Journal, The Waiting Room Reader, Global City Review, and The Coachella Review. Her poetry collection In the Zero of Sky was published by Assure Press in 2022, and she is working on a novel. She has performed her work in multimedia shows at a range of venues in New York City, where she lives. She dances samba and raqs sharki, teaches high school, and dilly-dallies with friends and family when not writing.

15. PICNIC AT THE MUSEUM

cypresses sway like
waltzing lovers, but
I wonder what
biocentric they
"feel,"
as the wind does not
whistle, it just is,
and the grass does not
velvet, but
the linen and the villa
whisper whilst
concrete sheep and
catered pillar, grassless
checked clover under,
seeming mundane in
sun, the speckled egg,
the blanket oven
roasted in woven wonder,
rays boasting.

the blanket oven
roasted in woven wonder,
rays boasting.
-Stasha Cole

STASHA COLE

Stasha Cole is a PhD candidate in literature. After completing her term as the co-editor of Stylus Journal of Art & Writing, she just began as an editorial assistant for Nimrod International Journal. She has been published here and there. You can often find her wearing pleated trousers and asserting the whimsy within the mundane.

16. FRIEND'S STREAM

My hands cupped,
I fill them full
from a quiet stream.
I touch the quenching water to my lips,
and it chills my tongue.
My heart opens
as I drink of its friendship,
cooling my throat,
caressing my mind,
soothing my soul.
Half-closing my eyes,
I look into the calming stream,
I smile back at myself.
"Ahh, sweet stream," I whisper,
"never leave me to thirst."

R. OLAF ERICH

R. Olaf Erich lives a quiet life in Wisconsin, USA, with his furry family, Shadow and Skyler. He has been writing for decades and has several dozen poems published. He is dedicated to writing more and sharing more of his poetry with the world.

17. MY DIRTY BOOTS

Boots find me in winter,
uneasy upon fledging feet,
blood on Achilles, staining leather,
warming skin strikes a steady beat.

Boots find me in spring,
sore but refusing to be inert;
sun-filled leaves and daytime showers bring
twirling engravings out of imprinted dirt.

Boots find me in summer,
cheerful and daring on a trail,
surrounded by neon splashes of color,
a wandering character in nature's tale.

Boots find me in autumn,
soft as butter, shaped by my stride.
Even gait grows greater freedom;
these boots of mine become my pride.

Winter finds me in boots—
once more, I tie my laces,
seeking out never-before-seen routes,
all year round, persistent paces,
roaming to fairview places.

Boots *find me in summer,*
cheerful and daring on a trail,
surrounded by neon splashes of color,
a wandering character in nature's tale.
-Caitlin Niznik

CAITLIN NIZNIK

Caitlin is a writer from a small town often confused with much larger towns in Virginia. She teaches adults English and previously taught elementary school students. When Caitlin is hard at work not working on her current manuscript, she writes poetry and oil paints in her cabin in the woods. She is part of a writing club in Fredericksburg, VA, called Riverside Writers. She has been published in The Avocet and the anthology Reflections by the Riverside.

18. LEAF: EXCITING JUMP

"oh, what a fool, he fell in fall."
he left the tree; this leaf is free,
gets torn around and hurled about,
and meets the ground with quite some doubt.
he had a choice; he chose to jump.
his father's voice was getting numb.
the flight was fun; first, he felt fright,
but then he flew, his wings spread wide.

an echo dim crept up on him,
remembers it's not menacing.
a thousand times he made this leap
and cast himself into the deep,
and afterwards, he always knows
this was the reason why he rose.
Next spring again, he starts to rise,
forgets, jumps still, and earns this prize.

the flight was fun; first, he felt fright,
but then he flew, his wings spread wide.
-Paul Lange

PAUL LANGE

I'm a 22-year-old physics student from Germany. Nature is one of my main sources of inspiration, but I also like to touch on the profound mysteries of life.

19. RIVER LORE

I.   Meander

By the time I realized my mistake,
the water had already taken shape.
On the Niobrara, trees stretched to the birds
after I decided to stop fighting the current. I floated
until I forgot the comment my mother made—
something about being contrarian, probably. On the wide,
spreading water, there is no safe route to disengage.
The tube-coraller warned us about the rapids
this time of year. Last week, he saw a naked
woman floating past the pull-off point.
She was found later that week, sun-swept
and bloated—filled to the scalp with water—
bending with the reeds. I lost a water shoe.

II.   Bend

Tantrums were cute when I was ten—thrown
grapes and spilled soda. "She just needs a nap."
Hangovers uglied on the water. I dug
my heels in the mucky riverbed and caught
a rock on my bare sole. The cluster of red, yellow,
and human drift around the bend. I can breathe
now, even when I dip my head under the surface
for silence. When rapids came, I lifted
my feet and let the blunted edges scratch my back.

III.   Reach

I didn't mean to
make them scream.
Soft sand dunes
called for my body
and let my spirit
roam. I speak to the trees

in the evenings,
who keep to themselves
in the morning.
I catch oncoming beer cans,
persuade the litterers'
rafts into the tall grass
where snakes
like to sleep. I splash
drying turtles.
I find grapes and a water shoe,
hidden in the opaque
current, resting in an alcove.

KENDRA BOYD

Kendra Boyd earned her Bachelor of Fine Arts degree with an emphasis in poetry and fiction in the Writers Workshop program at the University of Nebraska, Omaha. She served on 13th Floor Magazine in Spring 2024 as Editor in Chief, overseeing four genre teams. She also served on The Linden Review in Spring 2023 as Senior Editor, leading a group of Assistant Editors. Her senior thesis, Nymphalidae, directed by Dr. Lisa Fay Coutley, was completed in spring 2024. You can find her poetry in Clockhouse, Bloodletter, Streetlit, and Midway Journal.

20. BALD TREE

The tree didn't look me in the eye
The tree tried to hide her eyes

The tree looked embarrassed
The tree looked ashamed,
As if someone has hurt her
As if someone has stolen her soul.

A beautiful girl, in blue dress passed by
without looking at the tree,
The tree got more upset
and more ashamed.

I asked the tree why are you
so empty? She wept.

An angry axe man came
disappointed, frustrated, in despair,
took it out on me, hit me again and again.
I begged him to stop but he said:
until your soul is gone, I won't stop
so he made me bald.

A *beautiful girl*, *in blue dress passed by*
without looking at the tree,
The tree got more upset
and more ashamed.
-*Kev Studio*

KEV STUDIO

Ihtesham Ali is a rural poet who writes poems just for the sake of poetry.

21. NIGHT IS UNDERWATER

Head in the Clouds
The sound of waves
crashing, ringing
in my ears—
oh, so loud!

The night is underwater.
The moon has drowned.
The stars are now captives of the ocean.
The night still looks young, though,

even if it's underwater,
fading away,
deeper and deeper
to the bottom,
into a forgotten place.

even if it's underwater,
fading away,
deeper and deeper
to the bottom,
into a forgotten place.
-MS B*lues*

M.S. BLUES

Mia Soto (AKA M.S. Blues) is an 18-year-old writer, editor, mentor, stoner, and SBNR advocate. Through her work, her objective is to raise awareness to issues that society tends to neglect, as well as represent her Mexican, Polynesian, Indigenous, and Queer communities. She's arguably the most decorated figure in the literary magazine community, having been published over 125 times and serving on multiple magazine staffs. She's currently an editor for the following magazines: The Amazine, Adolescence Magazine, The Elysian Chronicles, Hyacinthus Zine, Chromatic Stars Review, Low Hanging Fruit, Sister Time, and DICED magazine. She's also a poetry/prose reviewer for The Cawnpore Magazine. In addition, she's the co-editor-in-chief of The Beaulieu Gazette and Sorry! Zine, as well as the assistant editor-in-chief for Voices of Asylum. Lastly, she is the founder and editor-in-chief of The Infinite Blues Review. You can interact with her on Instagram @m.s.blues_.

22. THE SNOWDROP

There was a crowd, I recall, sometime, somewhere,
close to the edge of spring's fresh, green-burgeoned heath;
and cold winter's forest dark—I met you there.
A fresh blossom, virgin white, lonely beneath
the canopy of ancient oak, whose cold shade
could not becloud your so captivating shine,
made conspicuous amid the purple glade
of bluebells—a snowdrop, singular, divine.

TERRY MILLER

Nottingham England-based writer Terry Miller honed his writing skills as a creative director for a number of advertising and creative agencies. Lately, a successful game inventor, Terry, utilizes his skills to create evocative, funny, and sometimes disturbing poetry. Written in an accessible form, Terry's poetry is deceptively complex, often tackling topical issues and exploring deep emotional issues. Terry's poems have been featured in several international poetry anthologies.

23. THE SPIRIT OF MERMAIDS

There
is
a dwarf
planet called
Salacia, that
carries the spirit of mermaids.

There
is
a star
called Algol.
It is known as the
most evil star in the whole sky.

Next
month,
Algol
will connect
to Uranus and
Mars, creating a conjunction.

In
the
sign of
Taurus, at
twenty-one degrees.
Uranus rules sudden changes.

*In
the
sign of
Taurus, at
twenty-one degrees.
Uranus rules sudden changes.
-Eliza Scudder*

ELIZA SCUDDER

Eliza Scudder (she/her) is a writer who creates comics, flash fiction, short stories, and poetry inspired by her life. Her work has been featured in Oddball Magazine, Bombay Literary Magazine, Parliament Literary Journal, The Radical Notion, Anodyne Magazine, The Red Ogre Review, Miracle Monocle, In Parentheses, The Fib Review, Echoes of Culture, and Word Peace Journal.

24. LOVE LETTER

There is magic in being of a place.

A home for rootedness
and for returning.

My home is the coffee-ground leftovers of an ancient glacial lake,
where fossils become skipping stones,
and skipping stones become summers.

And enough,
stacked between sugar-cake autumns
and heady lilac springs,
lying dormant
under lake-effected winters,
becomes entire lifetimes.

And I could spend mine
slow-sipping from backyard fountainheads,
waiting until that special kind of twilight moment for the Waterfowl
Flyover,
listening to their great ancestral song,
calling me back again and again
to my home waters.

The way the night smells sweet,
inviting all the heat of the day to rise from thirsty ground
and rest in her boundless, starry arms.
Or when it is cold—
snow-angeled, looking up,
and how the falling makes you feel like flying—
nothing but sky and snow and the silent sound it all makes.
My home is Great Lakes,
waters lapping at the doorsteps of the people who guide me,
who shape me.

My home—

this great northern country,
who taught me to love and honor Nature
for the absolute force that She is.
With seasons that crash and demand us to sit back and watch—

whether we had other plans or not.

Oh, how I love the hidden waterfalls
and fantasy greens,
the magnificent seaways,
and the lakes that feel like oceans.

How from the Ontario bottom
to the very Adirondack tip-top of my heart,

I am of this place.

And it carries me,
no matter where I go.

Oh, how I love the hidden waterfalls
and fantasy greens,
the magnificent seaways,
and the lakes that feel like oceans.
-Ashley Demar

ASHLEY DEMAR

Ashley DeMar is a writer, actor, recording artist, and arts educator originally from New York, now living on a tree farm in western North Carolina. Most recently, her work was selected for publication with the Black River Review, and—for the third year in a row—her poetry has appeared in the Adirondack Center for Writing's PoemVillage installations in Saranac Lake, NY. She has also been published in the WinglessDreamer anthologies My Cityline (where her poem "Oh, London!" was a top finalist), The Misty Cauldron, Erotica of Eternity, and Breath of Love. In 2021, her work was chosen to be part of the U.S. debut of the 'Of Earth and Sky' outdoor exhibition and its corresponding poetry anthology in Charlotte, North Carolina. Find her on social media @ashtreeofthesea to follow along for more updates on words and wanderings.

25. AT THE ALTAR OF THE BLACKBERRY BUSH

There is a great divining truth to blackberry picking.
And not yet dark,
the white moon of absolution shines forth,

giving testament to little things:
that bit of red pulp in purple cluster,
the brown spider wolfing its way through

blade and stalk, or the June bug
with rump against rump,
nestled in leafy crevasse.

These are nature's musings
in the twilight of reaching
round a jawline of thorns

to harvest the fruit of Phoenician hue,
while the twitter of swallow and seesaw sound
of mourning dove

serenade my pluck and prick.
And what crimson fluid baptizes
the storied leaves upon this swaying
stalk? The bowed and fruited bush
that thirsts for sacrificial bleeding.
It is the heyday of bursting baskets

and scratched skin, just there
beneath the nail, guarded by a bit
of armor too small to stay the

cordial of my efforts that cascades
down to the yellowed turf and the
den of beetle, an annual bloodletting

required before cobbler or jam

can set table. As I suck the source,
the blackberry awaits its desserts.

KHALIL ELAYAN

Khalil Elayan is a Senior Lecturer of English at Kennesaw State University, teaching mostly World and American Literature. His poems have been published in many journals including, The Black Fork Review, About Place Journal, and The Esthetic Apostle. His most recent short story was shortlisted and published in the Vincent Brothers Review Short Story Contest journal edition Housekeeping. Khalil focuses on subjects of trauma, nature, and climate change.

26. VENUS FLY TRAP

He could fee her heart breaking
in wordless astonishment
when he declined to be
her guiding star.

Knowing he could keep
no secrets from those eyes,
yet feeling the weight
of her scrutiny,
they stood in a standoff
just shy of open war.

His cerebral cortex's
compass needle
knew he did not merit
being mythologized
in her field of dreams
for he was completely bereft
of all domestic instincts.

Chiseled like stone
with substantial hands, jaw
and wrist bones,
he seldom was able
to walk a path of moderation.
Forever roaming new pastures,
he never missed being attached
to any one person or place or thing.

Though his love for her
was strong and ferocious,
he knew he would relish
the satisfactory sound
of domestic demolition
when "domestic" came to mean
duty bound.

Being one to notice
what others often do not,
he knew she belonged
where she was,

raggedly serene and
highly impervious
to all but a life
of houseplants and words.

Being the perpetual Dionaea Muscipula
that he was, he gracefully, fluidly
moved away.
Just an empty space
inside starched shoulders,
forever in search of
his next Venus fly trap.

BRENDA MOX

Brenda Mox is a poet and visual artist from Virginia. Her work has been published in Wingless Dreamer, Bewildering Stories, Down in the Dirt, Blaze Vox, Ariel Chart, Neo Poet, Discretionary Love, Corporeal, Heart and Mind, Edge of Humanity, Poetry Pacific, Poetry for Mental Health, Postcards from Young Unicorns, The Amazine, BarBar journals, Eber and Wein Anthology, Eastern Sea Bard Anthology.

27. THE BIGUOUS WORLD WIDE WEB

If mushrooms are people
Then fungi is god
A process that branches, fuses, and tangles
With the most prolific water, father of us all

The ingenuity of relationships
From animal, to human, to ant
Romans prayed to the gods
Of mildew but famines happened anyway

Plants learned to depend on fungi
They communicate with creativity
And with humor in the forest
Dispelling all illusions

Sloths die, humility sets in
Fungi happens, the neon god
We made is less than bacteria
In your gut, which is more

Than all of the stars in the galaxy.
So don't fret, you minus al person
Because there is so much more
Than all of these brainiacs.

ANN PRIVATEER

Ann Privateer is an artist, photographer, and poet. She grew up in the Midwest and now lives in California. Some of her recent work has appeared in Third Wednesday and Voices to name a few.

28. PITCHED

Sulphur impedes my taste,
And ivory envelopes my heart.

I gasp.
Yet under this wind it sounds like a whisper.

Pulling me tight, I hear you say.
"It'll be over soon"

You'd feel a shiver down my spine.
But by now it's just a mist.

I can smell something, it's almost sweet.
But I cannot find it in me to breathe.

Wax drips down my chest.
I'd complain about the burning,
But your eyes are twice as hot.

Do you remember when I danced with the trees?
And when you could sing with the birds?
I swear they followed your tune, a chorus of the blind.

RILEY STEWART

Riley Stewart was born and raised in Hamilton, Ontario, and has been writing poetry since the age of 12. He pursued an education in botany, falling in love with the natural world. Now that he's a fresh college graduate, he's found more time to pursue his personal hobby in the arts, writing poetry and stories. He hopes one day to become an established poet, with a collection of anthologies published of his works. Instagram: @RileyWithAQuill

29. HUNTED

feel it all.

feel it,
and then fold it up.
tuck it away like starched linens
in kitchen drawers.

the seasons change as childhood wallpaper,
new pictures with each new year
but the room
remains the same.

I watch all day,
strange weather.
stranger all the time.

I'm tired of waiting for the heat to turn to fall,
tired of waiting to remember
how to forget.

a tiger crouches in the snow,
spills blood like strawberries.

what was your name?
where did you go?

I dream about the last time we spoke
I dream about it every night for a year
I see a figure in your window
I see red on the ground.

I *dream about the last time we spoke*
I *dream about it every night for a year*
I *see a figure in your window*
I *see red on the ground.*
-Emily Couves

EMILY COUVES

Emily Couves is a multidisciplinary artist and writer living in Vancouver, BC.

30. IMPENETRABLE

Is the beady stare
of my porch chameleon
perched frozen in plain sight

not daring to budge a nimble body
holding suction
implanted feet

hair triggering bristly follicles
arching
exaggerations of immobility

dilating circular eyes
swooning
intentional navigation

away from my
looming
curiosity

a lizard pulse
flinches a blur
over wooden beams

sideway rolls
into a
minute crack

stops to hold my eyes
with an upside down
reptilian stare

foreign souls mirror
a glossy, watery, colorful
glance...impenetrable.

$ax^2 + bx + c = 0$

Is the beady stare
of my porch chameleon
perched frozen in plain sight
-Richard Pettigrew

RICHARD PETTIGREW

Surfer poet from Hawaii has had 2 plays produced and 11 poems published. Aloha

WRITE. FEEL. PUBLISH

NEVER GIVE UP ON YOUR DREAMS.

IT'S NEVER TOO LATE

If you liked our work, kindly do give us reviews on Amazon.com/winglessdreamer. It will mean a lot to our editorial team. You can also tag or follow us on social media platforms:

Instagram: @winglessdreamerlit @ruchi_acharya

Facebook: www.facebook.com/winglessdreamer

Mail us: Editor: editor@winglessdreamer.com

Sales: sales@winglessdreamer.com

Website: www.winglessdreamer.com

You can also support our small publishing community through donation:

www.paypal.me/Winglessdreamer

WRITE AND WRITE, AND SET YOURSELF FREE.

BOOKS PUBLISHED BY WINGLESS DREAMER

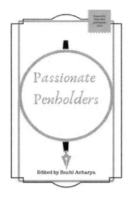

Passionate Penholders

Passionate Penholders II

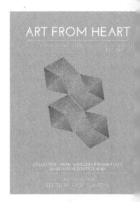

Art from heart

Daffodils

Father and I

Sunkissed

Tunnel of lost stories

Overcoming Fear

The Rewritten

BOOKS PUBLISHED BY WINGLESS DREAMER

uits of our quarantine   Magic of motivational   Diversity

rk Poetry Collection   A glass of wine with Edgar   Heartfelt

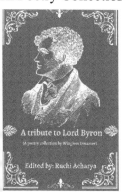

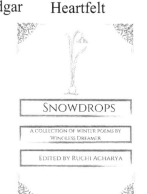

ibute to Lord Byron   Wicked young writers   Snowdrops

BOOKS PUBLISHED BY WINGLESS DREAMER

 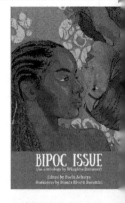

The Wanderlust Within   Writers of tomorrow   BIPOC Issue

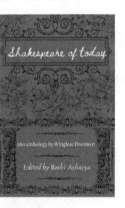 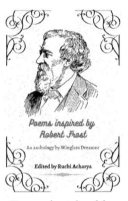 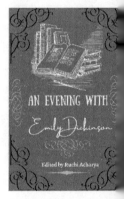

Shakespeare of today   Poem inspired by Robert Frost   An evening wit' Emily Dickinso'

It's time to snuggle up   Depths of Summer   Flee to Spring

BOOKS PUBLISHED BY WINGLESS DREAMER

  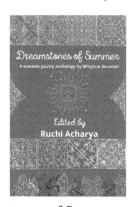

How to stay positive　　It's twelve o clock　　Dreamstones of Summer

 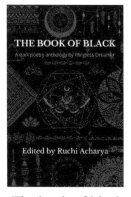 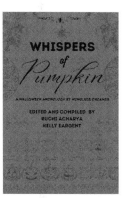

Dawn of the day　　　The book of black　　Whispers of Pumpkin

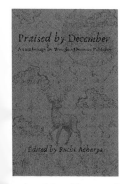  

raised by December　　Calling the beginning　　Snowflakes and
　　　　　　　　　　　　　　　　　　　　　　　　　　Mistletoes

BOOKS PUBLISHED BY WINGLESS DREAMER

My Cityline

My Glorious Quill

Garden of poets

Let's begin again

Field of black roses

Erotica of eterni

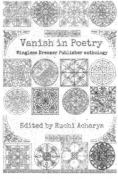
Vanish in Poetry

Oxymorons and Poets

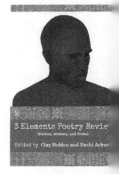
3 Elements

BOOKS PUBLISHED BY WINGLESS DREAMER

Still I rise

Mother, a title just above queen

Ink the Universe

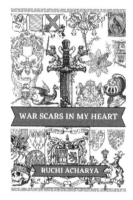

War scars in my heart

The Black Haven

I Have a Dream

Midsummer's Eve

Sea or Seashore

Summer Fireflies

BOOKS PUBLISHED BY WINGLESS DREAMER

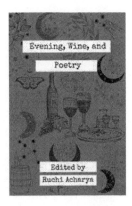

Evening, Wine, and Poetry

My Unheard September

Unveil the Memories

Paranormal Whispers

Dulce Poetica

Christmas Cheerios

My Sanskriti in Teal

Wings of Wonder

Growth in Grief

BOOKS PUBLISHED BY WINGLESS DREAMER

  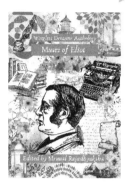

The Petal Pages   Unheard Phantoms   Muses of Eliot

reamer's Chronicles   The Sufi Under the Mystical Moon   Verses from the Rainbow

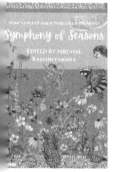 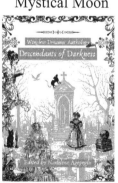 

nphony of Seasons   Descendants of Darkness   All Hallow's Eve

BOOKS PUBLISHED BY WINGLESS DREAMER

Soulful Verses

It's Crystal Clear

Enchanting Winter

Love Chronicles

Hearts in Orbit

Breathing Poetry

Into the Gloom

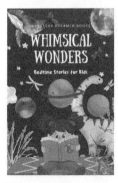

Whimsical Wonders

Hey there, Delilah!

BOOKS PUBLISHED BY WINGLESS DREAMER

Verses and Vignettes

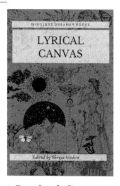

Lyrical Canvas

Time ticks, time heals

Mother's Reverie

Voices from the trenches

Echoes of Culture

Night Worship

The Silver Lining of
Heartbreak

Roots &
Leaves

BOOKS PUBLISHED BY WINGLESS DREAMER

Unfolding Colours

Dreamscapes and Daydreams

Petals & Pines

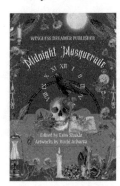

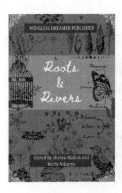

Pen's Palette

Midnight Masquerade

Roots & Rivers

Made in the USA
Columbia, SC
08 January 2025

51362240R00046